Essential Question
How can a pet be an important friend?

Too Many Pets?

by Michael McDade

illustrated by Viviana Garofoli

This is my family. There are five people in it.

The rest of my family
are pets. We have ten
different pets.

The cats are here when we move in.

"Please, can we keep them?" my sister asks.

My parents decide they can stay.

My sister loves the cats.
She names them Ted
and Betty. They sleep in
her room.

Then, our neighbors give us a gift.

"Now we have four pets," says Dad. "That's a lot of pets!"

Tick and Tock are cuddly.
Tock stares at me when
he wants a carrot.

Next, my friend gives us Freddy. Her family is moving to an apartment. It doesn't have room for a dog.

"Not another pet," says Mom.

I have a great relationship with Freddy. He likes to run and play. We are best friends.

Then one day, some
chickens show up. They
find a proper spot and
move in.

"No more pets!" says Dad.

"It's okay," says Mom.
"We can trade the eggs
for other things."

Margo is a duck. She
lands on the pond one
day. She likes the chickens.

Margo follows Dad. They have a great friendship.

"Too many pets!" says Mom.

This is how our family grew.
But wait! What's that
sound?

I glance in the closet.
I think we have four more
pets now!

Respond to Reading

Summarize

Use details to summarize *Too Many Pets?*

Character	Setting	Events

Text Evidence

1. How do you know *Too Many Pets?* is fiction? Genre

2. Where will the chickens live? Details from illustrations will help. Use Illustrations

3. What is the meaning of *apartment* on page 8? Sentence clues may help. Sentence Clues

4. Write about the pets in the story. Use illustrations to help.

Compare Texts
Read about a dog who is a friend.

My Dog Loves Me

I love my dog,
And my dog loves me.

When I'm at school,
He waits by the tree.

When I come home,
He runs all around.

He barks and he leaps.
He jumps off the ground!

He sleeps by my bed,
The last thing I see.

I love my dog,
And my dog loves me.

Craig Veltri/Photographer's Choice RF/Getty Images, illustration: Keiko Motoyama

 Make Connections

How can pets be friends?

Essential Question

How is this dog like Freddy?

Text to Text

Focus on
Literary Elements

Rhyme Words that rhyme have the same ending sound.

What to Look For In the poem "My Dog Loves Me," the words *me* and *tree* have the same ending sound. What other words rhyme in the poem?

Your Turn

Write a poem about an animal that is your friend. Can you use words that rhyme at the ends of some of the lines?